Remember:

I have placed My bow in the clouds, and it will be a sign of the covenant between Me and the earth.—Genesis 9:13

Read:

You can find the whole story of Noah in Genesis 6–9. You'll hear the exact directions God gave to Noah for building the ark. You'll see the animals that came aboard with Noah and his family. You'll learn how the birds helped Noah to know when the land was dry enough to leave the ark. But most important, you'll read the true meaning of the rainbow and God's promise to us all.

Think:

1. How do you think Noah felt when God asked him to build an ark?
2. What do you think Noah's family said to him?
3. What would you say if God had asked you to build an ark?
4. What do you think Noah and his family learned after the flood?
5. What can you learn from Noah's decision to obey God?

Do:

Make a Rainbow Reminder

1. On a white sheet of paper, write (or ask an adult to write) the memory verse above.
2. Cut around the verse in the shape of a cloud.
3. Using construction paper (or coloring white paper with crayons), cut one strip each of red, orange, yellow, green, blue, and purple.
4. In the order listed above, tape or glue the colors to hang from the bottom of the cloud.
5. Hang your Rainbow Reminder in the window or someplace where it will always remind you of God's promises.

Remember, even when there are rain clouds,
God's promises last forever.

Copyright © 2014 Anno Domini Publishing
www.ad-publishing.com

Text copyright © 2014 Renita Boyle
Illustrations copyright © 2014 Honor Ayres

Editorial Director: Annette Reynolds
Art Director: Gerald Rogers
Pre-production Manager: Krystyna Hewitt
Production Manager: John Laister

Printed and bound in Malaysia

Not a Cloud in the Sky

by Renita Boyle and Honor Ayres

There was not a cloud in the sky.

There was no sign of rain—no drip, no drop, no plip, no plop, no wind across the plain. But Noah built a boat anyway because he knew what God had planned.

No one believed what God said anymore.
Everyone forgot—everyone but Noah;
Noah did not!

"I made a wonderful world," God said, "and people to get along. Now they do all kinds of evil things and everything's gone wrong. Although it makes Me very sad, I'm going to start again.

There's going to be a **great big flood,** and I need your help, old friend. We're going to build a **great big boat:** I'll tell you what to do. Your family will be safe on board and lots of animals too!"

10

So Noah and Mrs. Noah, their three sons and their wives, they all began to build the boat that would one day save their lives.

Bang, bang went the hammer.

Zip, zip went the saw.

Up, up went the great big boat, so tall and long and wide, with a roof, a door and windows, and lots of rooms inside.

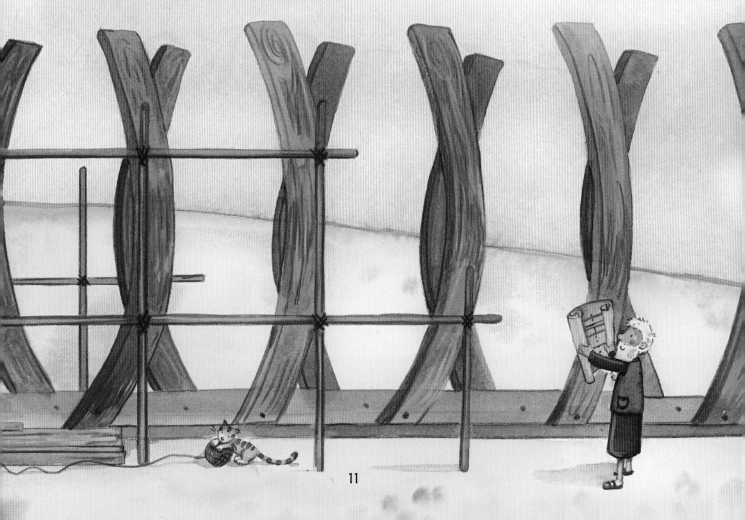

It took years and years to build that boat.
People laughed at Noah and stared.

"Trust the Lord and come on board,"
said Noah. But no one really cared.

"You're crazy!" they all said.
"What you say is a lie!
How can there be a flood when
there is not a cloud in the sky?!"

Then one day, when the work was done,
a cloud appeared and covered the sun.

Animals came from all around:
short and **tall**, thin and **round**.
Some were smooth and some were hairy;
some were sweet and some were **scary!**

Crawling, hopping, flipping, flopping, they marched and scampered and flew. Two by two by two by two, they marched and scampered and flew up the ramp and through the door, across the squeaky, creaky floor, into the many rooms inside the great big boat, so tall and long and wide.

Noah's family settled in too.

The more the clouds gathered, the darker it grew, until it was dark as darkest night. *Ba boom!* went the thunder. The door **banged** tight.

Plip, plop on the pointy roof; *drip, drop* against the door. *Flish, flash, splish, splosh, splash*, it pittered, it pattered, it poured!

For forty days and forty nights, rain thrashed down from the sky— but all inside the bobbing boat stayed warm and safe and dry.

Sometimes they were queasy.
Sometimes they were scared or bored.
But day after day they prayed and prayed
and chose to trust in the Lord.

They took care of each other and the animals too.
They did the work that God gave them to do.

Then one day, the rain just stopped.

God sent a breeze to blow, and slowly, slowly, very slowly, the water began to go. But months and months and months went past before the world was dry at last.

And though the wait was very long,
Noah's faith was very strong because
he knew what God had planned.

Old Noah laughed and skipped
and jumped when at last
they bumped on to dry land!

Up went the window, in came the sun, out went a dove to find dry ground. The dove came back with a branch from a tree.

"Hooray!" said all Noah's family.

And when God said, "Come on out!"
All of the animals gave a shout—roaring,
crowing, squeeking, chirping, buzzing,
howling, grunting, purring.

Crawling, hopping, flipping, flopping,
they marched and scampered and flew.

Two by two by two by two, they marched
and scampered and flew across the floor and
out of the door into the world so new.

Then Noah, Mrs. Noah,
their three sons and their wives
stopped to thank their amazing
God for saving all their lives.

In the sky above them,
a rainbow began to shine.

"I'll never flood the whole earth again,"
God promised. "Every rainbow will be a sign."

They left the ark on Mount Ararat to start
their brand new life.

Noah looked up beyond
the rainbow: there was
not a cloud in the sky.